Because I am a Girl

I can change the world

Rosemary McCarney
with Jen Albaugh
and Plan International

Second Story Press

Library and Archives Canada Cataloguing in Publication

McCarney, Rosemary A., author
Because I am a girl : I can change the world /
by Rosemary McCarney ; with Jen Albaugh and Plan International.

Issued in print and electronic formats.
ISBN 978-1-927583-44-9 (pbk.).—ISBN 978-1-927583-45-6 (epub)

1. Girls—Developing countries—Social conditions—Juvenile literature.
2. Girls—Developing countries—Biography—Juvenile literature.
I. Albaugh, Jen, 1973-, author II. Plan (Organization), author III. Title.

HQ777.M33 2014   j305.23082'091724   C2014-903821-6

C2014-903822-4

Editor: Kathryn Cole
Cover: © Shona Hamilton/Plan
Design: Melissa Kaita
Icons: © iStockphoto

Thanks to Elizabeth Barker for her contribution on Farwa's story
Thanks to Paula Roberts and Wahn Yoon for helping Plan create a Manifesto for girls

Printed and bound in Canada

Second Story Press gratefully acknowledges the support of the Ontario Arts Council, the Ontario Media Development Corporation, and the Canada Council for the Arts for our publishing program. We acknowledge the financial support of the Government of Canada through the Canada Book Fund.

ONTARIO ARTS COUNCIL
CONSEIL DES ARTS DE L'ONTARIO
50 YEARS OF ONTARIO GOVERNMENT SUPPORT OF THE ARTS
50 ANS DE SOUTIEN DU GOUVERNEMENT DE L'ONTARIO AUX ARTS

Canada Council
for the Arts

Conseil des Arts
du Canada

MIX
Paper from
responsible sources
FSC® C103567
FSC
www.fsc.org

Published by
SECOND STORY PRESS
20 Maud Street, Suite 401
Toronto, ON M5V 2M5
www.secondstorypress.ca

Contents

When you see a girl's name followed by an asterisk (*), her name has been changed to protect her identity.

Because I am a girl...

...Those words can inspire us or haunt us. If you are a girl the world can be full of promise and possibility, or it can be a world of barriers and danger. Girls everywhere share both of these experiences. For girls living in poverty or in countries of conflict or where human rights abuses are a matter of everyday occurrence, the future can be very uncertain. Many girls will never live to see their dreams fulfilled and their potential realized. Many will be denied an education. They will often go hungry and have to work in unsafe conditions. They will be forced to marry too young to a person who is not of their choosing. They will become mothers when they are still children themselves.

In this book, you will meet girls from many parts of the world who share their stories with you. They are young people just like you, but circumstances have put them into situations that seem insurmountable. Yet they survive. Some even bring about incredible change. We hope you enjoy meeting them.

—Rosemary McCarney

Because I am a Girl Manifesto*

Because I am a girl...
I watch my brothers go to school while I stay home.

Because I am a girl...
I eat if there's food left over when everyone is done.

Because I am a girl...
I am the poorest of the poor.

AND YET

Because I am a girl...
I will share what I know.

Because I am a girl...
I am the heart of my community.

Because I am a girl...
I will pull my family out of poverty if you give me a chance.

Because I am a girl...
I will take what you invest in me and uplift everyone around me.

Because I am a girl...
I can change the world.

A manifesto is a written statement that makes the purpose or beliefs of an organization clear for everyone to see. This is Plan Canada's Because I am a Girl manifesto.

ANUPA
Nepal

When I was very little I used to watch my big brothers get ready for school. I loved to see them button up their white shirts that my mother washed every night so that the boys would have sparkling clean uniforms to wear. I couldn't wait until I was old enough to have my own school uniform and join them every morning. I longed to be able to read and write like they did. I knew I would be good at it. Maybe I would learn so fast I would catch up to my brothers. Maybe I could get better grades than they did and win a prize at school! I was full of dreams then. Sometimes, when no one was looking, I would take a piece of paper so I could practice printing the alphabet. But paper is expensive, and my brothers needed it for their lessons, so I always had to give it back. I didn't mind. Soon it would be my turn.

Then, one day when I was seven, a strange man came to our house and took me away to be a *Kamlahari* — a household slave. I didn't understand what was happening, but I can still remember the look in my mother's eyes when the man, my "master," took me away. I was scared and I cried. It didn't change anything.

Later I found out that my parents couldn't afford to feed me or send me to school. Also they had borrowed money from this man, and they couldn't pay him back. He said he would take me to work in his house instead of taking the money. My mother didn't want to let go of me. She held onto my hands so tightly! She would

Did you know...

The Kamlahari system is a practice of domestic slavery that is in fact illegal in Nepal today, although it is still widespread. It exists in similar form in many parts of the world. There are an estimated 21 million people living as slaves in the world today. Every December 2nd is the United Nations International Day to End Slavery.

be upset if she could see my hands now. The soaps I have to use for the cleaning and laundry have burned them.

Here I try to hide my feelings, especially when I'm scared, but I still cry a lot. The nights are the hardest. I am so tired I can hardly hold my head up at the end of the day, but I still can't fall asleep. My "bed" is a mat and a thin blanket on the mud floor of my master's kitchen. Every night I shut my eyes and try to imagine that I am at home with my little brother sleeping beside me and my older brothers talking in the distance. My baby brother isn't so little anymore, and he'll be going to school now — because he was born a boy. When I think about all the things I have missed because I can't live at home, I feel so alone. I wish I could be there every day to help my brothers as they grow up into men, and to help my mother with all her work. When I first left our home to come here, I was so small that I couldn't reach the cook stove, and my mother said I had to wait until I was older to help her. But on my very first day here, my master told me to cook his dinner and handed me a chair to stand on.

It's very hard to see the master's children studying and playing. I've had to act like a grownup ever since I arrived. I take care of the children, even though I am not much older than they are. They don't have to cook all the meals, wash the floors and the clothes, boil the water, and do all the cleaning.

They don't have to jump up when the master needs fertilizer for his crops. He makes me collect cow dung from the roads. I don't want to do it, but I would be in for a beating if I said so. He yells at me and calls me horrible names for no reason. He's so big, and everything about me seems to make him angry. I am thankful to be back sleeping in the kitchen tonight. When I had my first period, he made me sleep behind the house in the cowshed for a week because he said I was dirty.

When will I ever be allowed to go home? I'm so afraid that I will have to live and work here forever. Will my dream of going to school and getting an education ever come true? Or must I remain a Kamlahari forever — just because I am a girl?

After eight years of domestic slavery, Anupa was freed. She is now 20 years old. Supported by Plan, she was able to complete an entrepreneurship course and now runs her own small animal pharmacy (selling medicine for farm animals, seeds, and fertilizer). Her income helps to support her family as well as the schooling of her younger brother. She is also in the 12th grade at school. She wants to continue on to university and study veterinary sciences or become a teacher.

Knowledge is power! The moment I returned home to my family I enrolled in school, and my skills improve each and every day.

9

Because I am a girl,
I was sent away
to be a household
slave. But because
I am a girl, I have
the ability to
empower others,
and can work
toward making
sure that all girls
are free!

Did you know...?

65 million girls around the world are being denied one of their most important rights — the right to learn.

The United Nations, a very important organization made up of most countries around the world, agrees that:

"All children have the right to a good quality education. They should be encouraged to go to school to the highest level they can."

So...why are millions of girls not in school?

There are many barriers that prevent girls from attending school and from learning while they are there. They include:

Kenya

Responsibilities at home

A girl's chores might include: caring for younger brothers and sisters, cooking/cleaning, and fetching water. Girls are often made to work for others in order to earn money for their families.

"If we have to get the water, we won't be able to go to school. It is very hard. I hope it rains soon."

— Mary and Sarah, 12 years old, Kenya

India

Poverty and the cost of going to school

In many countries, school is not free. Parents may not be able to afford tuition, uniforms, books, and supplies. Boys are often given the first opportunity to attend school.

"I dropped out of school when I was 12. My parents were facing financial difficulties…I had no choice."
— Munni*, 17 years old, India

Tanzania

Long distances from school

Many communities have few schools, and they are often a great distance from home, requiring girls to make long (and often unsafe) walks each day. Because there are not enough schools or teachers, many schools run in shifts. One group of students attends first, and a second group arrives when the first is done. By the end of the second shift, girls often have to walk home in the dark.

"Even though I don't enjoy the journey and sometimes find it very scary, I am willing to do whatever it takes to get a good education."
— Sylvia*, 8 years old, Tanzania

Early and forced marriage

1 in 3 girls in many countries is married before the age of 18. If this doesn't stop, there will be 140 million child brides by 2020. That would mean 39,000 girls married every day! Married girls are seldom allowed to go to school.

"I got married two years ago, while I was studying in Grade 5. I had to leave school. One day I wish to go back."
— Geeta, 15 years old, Nepal

Nepal

Bangladesh

Early pregnancy

About 16 million girls aged 15–19 give birth each year. Complications during childbirth are the leading cause of death for girls aged 15–24.

"I have a six-month-old daughter. I had a dream of studying to become a teacher....I would have liked that."
— Sonhita, 13 years old, Bangladesh

Violence in schools

Violence and sexual harassment in schools often cause parents to keep their daughters at home. Even in Canada, 1 in 4 girls reports being sexually assaulted before age 16. In some countries girls are forced by their teachers to trade sex for good grades.

Uganda

Yeukai (Zimbabwe)

Shannen (Canada)

"Not only boys, but also teachers use physical and sexual violence against girls. Many girls drop out of school to keep themselves safe."
— Hakima, 14 years old, Uganda

But girls' education is the key to breaking the cycle of poverty!

When girls are healthy, educated, and informed, they pull themselves, their children, and their communities out of poverty. Here is what can happen when girls have access to education.

With her elementary and secondary school education sponsored, Yeukai's dream was to become a lawyer so that she could fight for the rights of others. In 2009, Yeukai graduated from law school and currently works as a public prosecutor. In the future, she wants to set up her own practice and focus on child rights.

Shannen and the people of Attawapiskat (a Cree community in Northern Ontario, Canada), took the fight for a new school to the Canadian government after the original building was contaminated by a fuel leak. Their message resonated across the country — all children have the right to a school. Tragically, Shannen died in a car accident in 2010, but her passion inspired many to continue to work for the equality of children everywhere. And now there is a school in her community!

Marcela (El Salvador)

Marcela grew up in one of the most violent communities in El Salvador. Girls in her area often dreaded going to school because of the boys who would harass them or pressure them into sexual relationships. A few years ago, Marcela's school became part of a very important project — where young people work together to reduce violence against girls. Because of this, Marcela, aged 18, is still single, pursuing higher education, and using her knowledge to fight for girls' rights. She challenges gender stereotypes and works with various initiatives, including Because I am a Girl, to promote the importance of girls' education.

Education gives girls the chance to reach their full potential, to develop the skills, knowledge, and confidence to claim their rights.

"...let us pick up our books and pens. They are our most powerful weapons. One child, one teacher, one pen, and one book can change the world. Education is the only solution. Education first."
— Malala Yousafzai

United States

LUCY*
Zimbabwe

In my dreams, my whole family is sitting under the big mango tree, teasing each other and laughing. My mother tugs hard on my hair as she braids it, and I can hear the smile in her voice as she leans over my shoulder to whisper in my ear. "You must stay strong, Lucy, and listen to your sister." Wiping the sweet mango juice from my chin, I laugh, and promise her that I will mind Naomi's rules.

But when I wake up, I am alone. It is only my sister and I now. My father died when I was five years old, and my mother passed just a year later. She was HIV positive and became so very sick at the end. I would cry when I saw her in so much pain, I felt so helpless! Just a few days after my sixth birthday, she had a stroke. Naomi and I were on our own.

The big mango tree is gone, so is the food. Every morning, I wake up with pains in my tummy because I am so hungry. We don't usually have any food at home, and most days I have to go to school without eating. Naomi says that I have to train myself not to feel hungry until the end of the day, but that is really hard to do! Sometimes I can't concentrate during lessons, or I feel dizzy and fall asleep and the teachers punish me. While my friends are working hard in class, I'm thinking about what and where to get my next meal...or if I will eat at all.

My memories are so strong...I can still smell the big pieces of antelope meat that my mother would cook on the fire. I loved the sounds all around us when my father and the other men would come back from the hunt. The neighbors would all gather in our yard, and the women would sing as they prepared the meal for us all.

We don't have meat anymore — we just eat whatever we can find. Naomi says we should not ask for help from the neighbors — it is our job

I am a very hard worker, and don't mind washing dishes or doing the laundry for others. My sister works so hard to take care of us both, and I want to help as much as I can.

to take care of ourselves. Our other relatives did not want to take us in. Sometimes we will work for them, fetching water and firewood or washing their dirty dishes...even bathing their young children. We ask to work for food, but there are still times when we do not get to eat.

Sometimes our aunt, my father's brother's wife, will tell us to cook the family meal, and then send us to do other tasks while our cousins are eating. It is very hard to smell the wonderful dishes as they are cooking, and then be told to cover them up and serve them to the men! Only when the boys are full are we allowed to return. Often there is nothing left, and we are told to clear and wash the dishes.

Naomi tries very hard to take care of us both. She found a job at the local beer hall, but I worry about her working there. It's not a safe place for a girl, and she comes home very late at night. She's all I have and I don't know what I would do if anything ever happened to her. The fifteen dollars a month she makes is not enough for us to be able to eat every day and also pay my school fees. Sometimes we are very lucky and she is able to bring home some leftover food from the customers at the bar.

There are times when I skip school to find work I can do in exchange for food. The job I

We take turns collecting the water, but Naomi is much stronger than I am, and can balance the big bucket. I often have to make two trips.

hate the most is collecting firewood — it is very hard work, but that's not what bothers me. My arms and my legs get all scratched up, and I am scared to go into the dense bush by myself. There are times when the people that I work for will not give me anything to eat in return, and I wonder if they would treat a boy in the same way. But I don't let myself cry, no matter how hard things get. I made a promise to my mother, and I will keep it.

My teacher says that I am very bright! He knows that I would be doing better in school if we had more to eat at home. When he tells me that he's proud of me for trying my best to focus and participate in class, it helps me to stay strong. Many girls here have dropped out of school because they are just like my sister and me — they're orphans and have to take care of themselves. Sometimes they have to beg or steal, or sell themselves for food or money. It's not fair! But I think that getting an education is the best way for me to take care of myself... and others.

One day, I want to be a doctor. I am in Grade 6, so I have a long way to go, but I will do whatever it takes to make my dream come true. I won't give up. I know my mother is watching, and I hope that she is proud of me.

Did you know...?

The United Nations Convention on the Rights of the Child states that:

"You have the right to the best health care possible, safe water to drink, nutritious food..."

Did you know that the first 1000 days of your life are the most critical ones? And did you know that your brain has already grown to nearly 90% of its adult size by the time you reach the age of 3?

All through your childhood and teenage years, different parts of your brain are developing and making very important connections. Proper nutrition is the key to this growth and development. It's the fuel that keeps your brain running!

But around the world about 1 in 4 children under 5 years of age is stunted (their bodies and brains have not grown properly) due to a lack of proper nutrition.

Malnutrition (not having enough food, or not having the right kind of food for good health) exists all over the world.

So...what does that mean for girls?

▶ 17 million children are born underweight each year because their mothers are malnourished.

▶ Girls are 3 times more likely to suffer from malnutrition than boys.

▶ 7 out of 10 of the world's hungry are women and girls.

▶ In many societies, women and girls are victims of food discrimination (eating only what remains after male family members have eaten).

▶ Girls are often asked to give up their meals to feed their brothers.

It is estimated that nearly a billion people are undernourished, and more than 3 million children die each year because of hunger.

What does it feel like to be growing up hungry?

Ethiopia

"When you have been hungry for some time, you get stomach cramps and you get nauseous. You lose interest in everything around you. The last time there was a drought here, many of the children at my school went home before the end of the day to see if their parents had been able to get some food for the family."

— Amarech, 10 years old, Ethiopia

Kenya

When most of a family's income is spent on food, there is often not enough left over for things like medicine or school fees. When people have enough to eat, they can focus on their children's futures — especially when it comes to education and health.

Women and girls are affected greatly by hunger and poverty because of the status they are given in their homes and communities. But we know that women around the world are major food producers!

Yet, women are still much less likely than men to own or control the land where they grow the food.

Check out some amazing projects and people working toward the goal of having enough food for all people everywhere (global food security).

What percentage of the world's food is grown and sold by women?

▶ In Latin America, it is more than 30%

▶ In the Caribbean that number jumps to 46%

▶ In Asia, women produce 50–60%

▶ And in all of Africa that lies south of the Sahara Desert, women are responsible for 80–90% of the food grown and sold!

These Nicaraguan children are monitors, part of a food security network of nearly 600 young people. They are trained to teach people about proper nutrition, ways to access healthy food, and more productive farming methods.

Nicaragua

Sudan

In Southern Sudan and Kenya, the Food for Education project is greatly improving student enrolment and reducing the numbers of students who have to drop out each year. The project includes supplying a healthy meal during the school day and take-home food packages that girls can take home for themselves and their families. The girls also learn how to plant, care for, and harvest the food in their school gardens! School feeding programs help girls *get* to school and they help *keep* them there.

World Food Day

October 16th is World Food Day. The aim of the day is to raise public awareness of the world food problem and unite people to take action in the struggle against hunger, malnutrition, and poverty.

Philippines

FARWA

Pakistan

When we were little, my friend Sonia and I were so close we were like sisters. We were both poor, but when times were hard, we shared what we had. Whatever happened, we could count on each other and share a secret or a smile.

But when Sonia and I were twelve, she was forced to marry a forty-five-year-old man. She told me that he beat her and that she cried every night before she went to sleep. She knew that when she woke up he would beat her again. I cried, too, when she told me. For the first time ever, we couldn't make each other smile.

Then, when we were fourteen years old, Sonia gave birth to her first baby. She thought that once she was a mother, everything would be better. But she was wrong. The baby is healthy, but taking care of an infant is a lot of work, and Sonia is still a child herself — like me. And worst of all, her husband still punches her all the time. No one says or does anything to stop him. I want to help Sonia, but there's really nothing I can do. Sonia is his wife.

Sonia didn't choose to marry her husband — she didn't want to marry anybody then — but her parents, like mine, are poor. They couldn't afford to keep her, and he could. Most of the girls from my village are sold into marriage because when a man takes a wife, he has to pay her parents a bride price called a dowry. When parents don't have enough money to pay for food or shelter and have no other way to earn more, a dowry can seem like the only solution. But it seems to me that the girls are the ones who always end up paying, and the price is high. It costs them their dreams for the future. I don't understand. The boys our age are always outside playing or going to work to help their families. Girls aren't allowed to do that.

More and more of the girls I know have stopped going to school. Every day someone is missing. They are married off for the bride price and soon they will have children of their own. I shudder at the thought. Am I ready to have a baby? Some of the girls, who are even younger than Sonia and me, already have two or more children. It scares me when I think about it. Maybe I will be next. But I want to keep going to school, to keep learning. Why do the boys get better treatment? What makes us less worthy? Boys aren't any better, and girls aren't any worse!

I decided to ask those questions at the Children's Forum meeting, where children are allowed to speak to adults about important matters. Maybe I will get some answers. Another girl in my village, Saima, once asked the same questions. Saima was older than most when she had to get married; she was already fifteen. Like me, she loved to learn. She was the smartest girl in our school. Whenever the teacher asked a question, we all knew that Saima had the right answer. I don't think even Saima would have the answers I'm looking for.

When it came time for Saima to be married, her in-laws told her she could continue on with her education. We all thought she was lucky.

After many months of marriage, Saima felt she was ready to return to school. But her mother-in-law would not allow it. She beat her instead.

Did you know... ?
39,000 girls under the age of 18 are married every day. At the current rate, more than 140 million girls will become child brides by 2020, unless *we* do something.

No, she tortured her — a fifteen-year-old girl who simply wanted the chance to learn.

Saima never did go back to school.

Soon her first child arrived, a beautiful baby girl. But that was not what her husband wanted and he beat her mercilessly for her "mistake" — he wanted a son. I was afraid to have a fate like Saima's. I didn't want anyone to have a story like hers. But they will. And I might have too, except for someone very special.

When my turn came, I had just finished the 8th grade, and I was so proud of my accomplishment. I was one step closer to reaching my secret dream of becoming an engineer. But my parents told me they couldn't afford to give me any more schooling. I would have to get married instead. I would have to leave everyone and everything I cared about. I was so scared and so sad, I just wanted to hide away from the world.

But that was when my story changed. I got lucky. It's so rare to be lucky here. My aunt has offered to pay for me to go back to school. She sees that selling off young girls as child brides is wrong. It doesn't lift anyone out of poverty. She is doing what she can to change it, by starting with one girl. By starting with me.

That's what I do now, too. I try to stop child marriages, one little bit at a time.

I tell people all about it. I tell people in my village, I tell people in the government, I tell all sorts of people in the United Nations. I tell them this has to stop. Girls should have rights, and we will not let anyone deny us. Maybe others will join me when I speak and will add their voices to mine. We must speak up for what is right.

Maybe then, even if Sonia and I are old women by that time, girls will be free to make their own choices — and so will our granddaughters.

Youth delegate Rafick (from Malawi) and I are presenting the 'Take the Vow' petition (to end child marriage) to the UK's International Development Secretary, Justine Greening. The petition contained 10,000 signatures!

Did you know...?

1.4 billion people live on $1.25 a day. 70% of this group is made up of girls and women.

Why?

Mostly, it is because of a combination of poverty and discrimination against girls.

Though everyone in a family, community, or country is hurt by poverty, it is most deeply felt by girls because of the way they are viewed.

If a girl is born into a poor family, her parents might make a different set of choices for her than they do for her brothers. If she is last in line for food, health care, and education, then she's already at a disadvantage as she moves through the cycle of poverty. Without an education she won't have the skills she needs to get a good job, and marrying early might seem like her only option. An early pregnancy with little access to proper nutrition and health care is dangerous, and her children are more likely to live in poverty, repeating the cycle.

The great news is that we can break the cycle of poverty!

The importance of clean water

Clean water and living in a clean environment improves the health of a community.

Often, women and girls in poorer countries walk about 4 miles (6.4 km) a day and spend 15 hours each week getting enough water to carry home. If there was a well nearby, the problem would be solved. When less

Nepal

"We are poor. I had to drop out of school when I was in Grade 2. When I was 14, my family started talking about marriage, which I couldn't deny, as it is a tradition in our village. During my pregnancy I wasn't feeling well. I vomited and couldn't swallow anything except milk. Now, my baby boy isn't very healthy."

—Sabita, 16 years old, Nepal

Nepal

time is needed to fetch water, more girls can attend school! Clean water and sanitary conditions are very important to global health and ensuring that every girl is in school.

Did you know that more than 1 billion people around the world are forced to go to the bathroom in the open, and that contaminated water causes deadly diseases that kill 1 child every 20 seconds? There is actually a World Toilet Day, which is celebrated every November 19. It reminds us that poor sanitation is a huge global problem...one that we can solve!

Good health

A healthy mother and newborn are very important in breaking the cycle of poverty. Due to problems during pregnancy and childbirth, about 800 mothers die every day. It is hard to believe that is about one every 100 seconds. When mothers die, they are not there to protect their children, to fight for their rights, to ensure they survive and thrive.

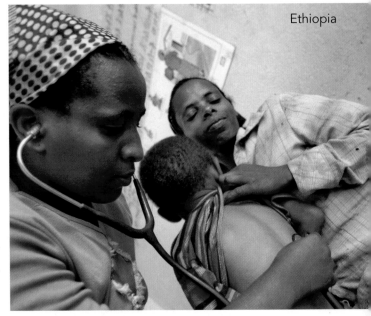

Ethiopia

Child protection

The countries that make up the United Nations agree that children have the right to protection from abuse, neglect, and exploitation. Girls everywhere are threatened by high levels of violence and abuse. Making sure that they are safe is a first step toward empowering them and making change.

Laos

Bangladesh

Benin

Burkina Faso VSLA

Stopping poverty

Families and communities need skills and knowledge so that they can overcome poverty. If we provide people, especially women, with skills and business training, they can run a farm or business more successfully. Helping communities to set up Village Savings and Loan Associations (VSLAs) is another way to help. VSLAs can give small loans to those who could otherwise not borrow money. With these loans, people, women included, can start a business or farm. Then they can earn money for themselves and their families. With education, training, and a small financial boost, girls everywhere are building successful businesses...and improving the lives of those around them!

Education is the key to breaking the cycle of poverty.

When girls are healthy, educated, and empowered, they will pull themselves and their children out of poverty. We see it happen all the time.

Myanmar

MARINEL

Philippines

Typhoon Haiyan changed everything that was familiar to me. It swept our house out to sea and tore the roof off our school. It took away people we loved. Sometimes I'm afraid it has taken away our future.

If the sun would only come out more often, it might feel like the storm was really over — like we were safe once again. But it still rains here a lot of the time. I can't sleep at night when I hear the rain splatting onto our "roof." Now that our home is really just four pillars, some wood, and a tarp, I can hear the plastic flapping around in the wind, and it makes me so nervous. I'm certain that another typhoon is coming. When I close my eyes I can still see the roofs of houses flying around in the storm. Sometimes in the mornings, I smell my mother cooking cassava. I never used to mind it.... Now it leaves a bitter taste in my mouth that reminds me of disaster and poverty. I guess that's because cassava was the only thing we had to eat for many days. Our crops were under water from the flooding and even if people had money, there was no food left to buy. People were very hungry and begged passing trucks to stop and share whatever food they might have.

We don't have a toilet anymore, so I have to go to my grandma's, which is a long walk from here. I also have to bathe outside with my clothes on. Sometimes men and boys walk by while I am washing, and I want to run and hide.

After the typhoon passed over us, we went out and looked everywhere for our clothes and books and pictures. We dug through piles and piles of wet rubble for anything we

Did you know...
Typhoon Haiyan destroyed more than a million schools and homes in the Philippines in just a few hours.

This is what my neighborhood looked like after Typhoon Haiyan hit us.

could salvage. Even if we found the smallest personal thing, it became very precious to us. I was so happy when I found the red first place ribbon I had won in an essay writing contest stuck between the rocks, carried there by the floodwaters. It reminded me of all the other awards I'd won in school. I used to hang my medals and ribbons on the wall in my room, my "hidden wealth," but all of that is gone now. All I managed to save was my English book, one notebook, my pen — and the ribbon. Even though it is dirty and tattered, it reminds me of life before so much was taken away. I promised myself that I would win another award one day — a sign that I would return and finish school.

We couldn't go to class for many weeks because the school was so badly damaged it was unsafe. And anyway, we had to spend all our time standing in line for food and blankets and medicine. Some of my friends dropped out of school for good. Now they go out fishing with their fathers every day instead. It makes me sad, because knowledge is power. Education gives you choices for your future. This storm took so many choices away from us — and I want to take some of those back! Now that the school is open again, I'm so happy! We have to work really hard to get caught up, but I know I can do it.

I don't have many things now; I'm just beginning again at the bottom. But the one thing I do have is my voice. I have always spoken out about issues that matter to me — I am one of the leaders of a children's group in my village. On the weekends we used to travel to other villages to work with the younger kids. We would talk to them about children's rights using games,

Did you know...

Girls are more likely to die in a natural disaster. In many countries girls don't learn to swim, may be kept isolated and uninformed, and may not be considered in communications designed to give early warnings about hurricanes and tsunamis.

39

I'm smiling because I know I am very lucky. I am still here, and I have my family. And I know that we have a better shelter than others in our village!

singing, dancing, and drawing activities. We would also put on performances that taught about climate change and our environment. And now, it's more important than ever to share what we know! I am alive today because many of us prepared and practiced what we would do in an emergency. There are so many things we can change about the way we are treating our earth, and so many things we can do to help save more lives if another disaster comes. We need to teach each other, to share our skills and knowledge, so that we can all be stronger. We really can decide our own future!

This is my mom! We both know how important it is for me to finish my education. No matter what it takes, I will finish school! As the roof isn't really fixed at the school, our books and work often get wet, but that won't stop me.

Did you know...?

HAPPY BIRTHDAY!

On October 21st, 2011, a baby girl was born in rural India, and welcomed as the world's 7 billionth person. Of course, there is no way to know exactly who the 7 billionth baby was, but Baby Nargis was one of the children chosen to be a symbol of this important moment in human history. Let's learn a bit more about Baby Nargis, and what she will face as she grows up.

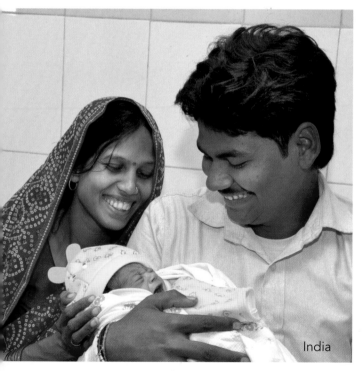

India

The story of Nargis

Nargis was born in a poor community. She is lucky to have been born safely at all. She may not have a chance to go to school, get a decent job, choose whom she marries, or how many children she will have. Millions of girls in the world are in the same situation.

If Nargis survives to age 5 and goes to school, she may continue within the cycle of poverty, or she may be able to grow and develop into a confident, healthy adult who can help empower other girls. Because she is a girl, she will share what she knows.

Nargis has come into a world where almost half of the population is under the age of 24. About 1.7 billion of those people are girls. If all of them were healthy, educated, and able to use their voices and assert their rights, just imagine what they could do!

Girls are half of the world's future — they will grow up to be leaders and creative thinkers. They will become human rights lawyers, doctors, teachers, inventors — whatever they wish to choose. With knowledge and energy, they will build a better, safer future for us all.

> "My mother used to listen to my brothers and not to me. I used to be afraid and never imagined I could do what I can do now. Now they all listen to me and I am treated like my brothers. I am the secretary of the school parliament. I want to be a children's doctor. I want to distribute all the experience and knowledge I have to other girls around the world."
> —Asalaa, 12 years old, Egypt

Cameroon

Fabiola is a student in rural Cameroon, and a member of the Youth Empowerment through Technology, Arts and Media project. She produces media that raises awareness and creates change around gender issues and girls' rights.

She's also created Girls on the Front, an association that helps girls to defend their rights at home and in their many different countries.

Germany

Members of the Action Youth Group in Germany wanted to come up with a way to communicate the importance of Universal Birth Registration to their government. They decided to collect individual fingerprints of over 400 students at a local school to symbolize the importance of identification.

These activists are getting their message across and sharing what they know one fingerprint at a time!

Around the world, 250 million children under the age of 5 are "invisible" because their births have never been recorded. That means getting medical help or registering for school can be impossible. If you do not have a birth certificate then you cannot be counted, and every kid counts!

Maureen is a member of the Hygiene Club in her school in Uganda. She has received health and hygiene training that she now shares with her fellow classmates and community.

Girls in her area often miss 4–5 days of school each month because of their menstrual periods. The Hygiene Club works to educate girls about their menstrual cycle and provides them with affordable, feminine hygiene products so that they don't have to miss school.

KATHRYN*

South Sudan/Uganda

One day while my parents were out and I was home alone with my two young brothers, we heard the sound we had learned to dread. Gunshots! The sounds of shooting got louder — closer and closer to our home — and we could hear people screaming. My brothers ran to me shouting, "We are dying, we are dying. Kathryn, we are dying." They held on to me so tightly, and I could feel them shaking. I didn't know what to do. I tried to be calm and told the boys to grab some clothes and food. We ran from our house, away from the sound of the guns, away from South Sudan. We did not even know where to go. My mother had talked once about a camp across the border in Uganda. I didn't know how far it was, but I hoped my mother would also try to go there. Many people, including children, were running, and we joined them. My friend, Emma*, was in the group. She was without her parents too, so we stayed together as we fled.

We walked about 125 miles (200 km) to reach the camp. We hid and slept in the trees and we were very hungry. A lot of children were crying as their mothers desperately looked for what to feed them in order to survive. Being in the forest in the middle of the night was scary — we could hear the wild animals. I still have nightmares, pictures that will never leave my mind. We saw the bodies of people who had been shot. We saw people drown in the rivers we had to cross. Emma and I tried to keep my little brothers from seeing them too, but I know they also have nightmares. Now we are refugees.

I still don't know where my mom is, and I don't know how to find her. Whenever new refugees arrive from South Sudan, I ask if they know or have seen my mother. Often I dream that she's here, and in those

My friend Emma would do anything to protect her younger brothers. We try to be both mother and father to our siblings, and to the other younger children here. But we are just kids ourselves. We need our moms and dads.

moments I am so happy! But each morning when I open my eyes, we are alone. At least I have my brothers and Emma. I am thankful for that. But I need my mom and miss her so much.

Life is very hard for us in the refugee camp. When we first got here, we had to sleep under a tree while we waited for help. Now we have a tarp over our heads. It isn't as good as a roof. Whenever it rains, the wind blows it so hard that we all get soaked. But at least it offers some shelter. I do my best to make a home for my brothers. I don't want them to know how worried I am about Mother and Father and about our future. Emma is just as worried about her parents, but she tries not to show it, too. Some people say the fighting is still bad in my village and many more people have been killed. They say that we may be here for a long time — maybe two years.

Everything is difficult here. We have to fetch water every day and find food, and pound the grain so we can cook and eat. Yesterday I spent the whole day in line at the borehole. We have only one borehole in the camp for seven thousand people, so women and girls start to line up in the middle of the night. Emma and I take turns standing in line. When it is my turn, I go quietly while my brothers are sleeping, but I worry about leaving them alone. Sometimes I have to leave my jerry can in the line so that I can run back to check on them. It can take as long as twelve hours of standing in line to get even a little water.

Even though we really need water, rain can be a bad thing. The ground is very dry and it takes time for water to sink in. We are in the lowlands, so when it rains, floods come quickly. Then we have to worry about the diseases we can get from dirty water. Sometimes we use communal pit latrines, and, as a girl, I am prone to getting infections because of poor hygiene in these facilities. I'm glad there are people in the camp who teach us what we can do to keep ourselves safe. More and more refugees arrive from South Sudan every day, and we are more crowded than ever. We need more doctors and more medicine here. I'm always afraid that my brothers, Emma, and I could get sick, or even die from a disease.

There's no school here. My mother was never able to go to school — South Sudan has been a country filled with war for the last thirty years. She wanted life to be different for my brothers and me.... She made sure we went to school. Now what I want most is for all of us to be able to go to school here. I teach the younger children things I know. I have to make sure my brothers keep learning. They are my responsibility now.

I do the best I can to make the refugee camp a home for my brothers and for the other young ones here. There is no one shooting at us now, but sometimes I think I still hear the sounds of those rifles firing at people outside our home. I don't know if we will ever see our parents again. More than anything I just want to go home to our village...to be with the rest of my family and see my school friends. But we are here, and we are alive. All I can do right now is to be a friend to Emma and a mother to my brothers until we can find our mother...until we can go home — *if* we can ever go home again.

Until then, it's my job to be the heart of our community, because I am a girl.

Did you know...?

By now, you know about the difficulties that girls face in many parts of the world. You have also read about some of the amazing ways that girls and women, men and boys are overcoming those problems. As hard as it may seem, the cycle of poverty can be transformed into a cycle of opportunity! Here are a few of the ways people of all ages are making change, right at the very heart of their own communities.

GRANDMA POWER!
(Girls of all ages)

In 160 villages across Benin, more than 12,000 grandmothers are battling malnutrition!

In Benin, West Africa, 1 in every 3 children suffers from a constant lack of nutritious food (chronic malnutrition). The Benin Community Nutrition project focuses on training and organizing grandmothers to help change old habits and make better decisions within their communities.

Those grandmothers certainly are the heart of their communities! They've empowered themselves, and the generations that will come after

Benin

them, to make changes that will directly affect the future of their families, villages — their entire country in the long run. The nutrition project was designed around knowledge that village people trust grandmothers and look to them for their wisdom and advice, just like you trust your own grandmothers!

> *"Grandmothers have a huge impact on communities. They are consulted, and they influence decisions in the family. They have power and knowledge, and they are keen that their communities benefit from them."*
> —Roch Mongbo (Secretary of the Benin National Food and Nutrition Council)

WEDDING BUSTERS!
(Boys and girls working together to end child marriage)

In Bangladesh, 66% of girls are married before they are 18. In an effort to change this, a children's organization works with their local government and community to create "child marriage free zones." Boys and girls in this group work together, calling emergency meetings whenever they hear that a child marriage is being arranged. They visit the parents to discuss the issue and the negative results that an early marriage could have on their daughter. If that doesn't work, they tell the authorities.

India

We've watched women and girls transfer improvements in their own lives to the lives of their children, families, and communities. In more than 80 communities in India, volunteer health workers and Trained Birth Attendants (TBAs) have helped mothers to have safer births and healthier children. They also educate the people of their villages about adolescent and reproductive health and HIV awareness.

Bangladesh

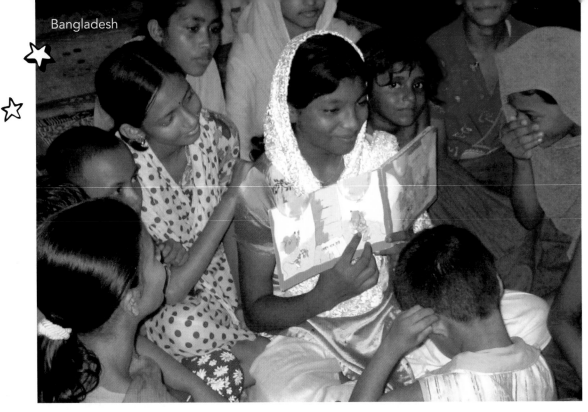

Amena (above) grew up living in the streets of Bangladesh. From the age of 4, her job was to collect any rice that fell on the ground in the market, so that she and her mother could have something to eat. Social workers took her to a Drop-In Center (DIC) in Dhaka. She's now in Grade 7, going to school regularly, and doing very well! Amena's interest in education has led her to spend time helping other children at the center learn to read. Many of the girls at the DICs in Dhaka feel that it is their duty to invite children in the community to come in off the streets. Their lives and futures have changed drastically since coming to live there, and they want all children to have the most basic of rights — safety, food, education... and most of all, a home. Tania, Shumi, and Shahida (right) are three such girls. One of the most important rights that Drop-In Centers provide to the many children in their care is the right to a name and a nation — in the form of a birth certificate. A birth certificate means that a child has a legal identity. Without it, a child is "invisible," uncounted, and has no rights.

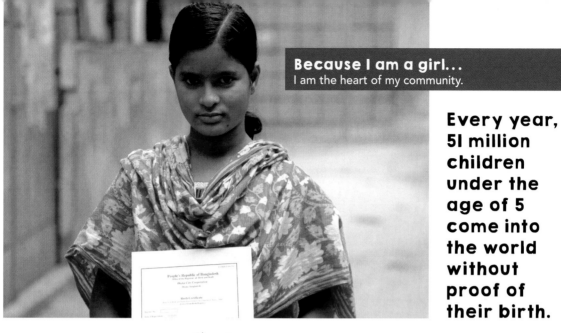

Every year, 51 million children under the age of 5 come into the world without proof of their birth.

Shumi

Shahida

57

Tania

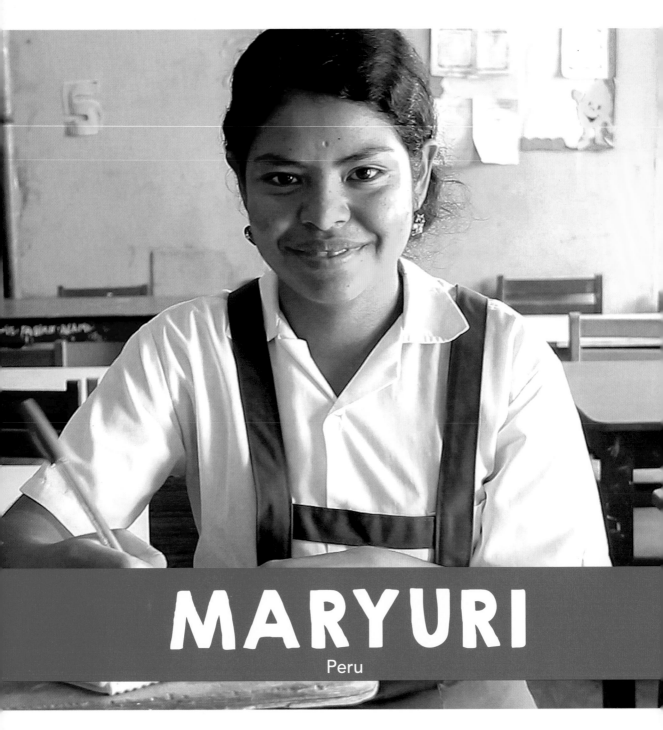

MARYURI

Peru

I will never forget the day my father took me out of school. How could I forget it? It was one of the worst days of my life. It was as if he'd locked me in a room and turned off the light. I could feel my dreams slipping away. Without an education, I would never be able to reach my goals.

I could understand why he did it — he was trying to protect me. Several girls in my school had become pregnant at the age of thirteen or fourteen, and he was worried that would happen to me. I begged and I pleaded for him to trust me. I tried to convince him that all I wanted was to learn. But he had made his decision — I was to stay home.

Every morning I would look out the window and watch some of the other girls pass by on their way to school. I wanted so badly to run outside and join in, to link arms with them and tell stories as we walked. But I had to stay and watch them disappear into the distance without me. All I had at home were three school notebooks, and I would pull them down off the kitchen shelf every night to study my old notes. After a while this was making me so heartsick that I made sure I was nowhere near the front window in the mornings. My notebooks started to gather dust on the shelf.

Then, one day when my father was away, one of the teachers from my school came by to ask my mother why I was no longer coming to classes. The two of them whispered together for a very long time. I really wanted to hear what they were saying, but I had to wait outside with my imagination running

Did you know...?
65 million girls of school age are not in school. Sometimes the reason is simple — parents want to protect their daughters from school-related gender-based violence and outside influences they cannot control.

wild and my patience growing thin. Finally, they came outside with big smiles on their faces. I don't know how the teacher did it, but she managed to convince my mother that I should go back to school! And somehow, a day later, my mother managed to convince my father. I knew that this decision would change my life for the better, but we had no idea how quickly some of those changes would come.

When I returned to class, I learned that a new program had begun in our school to teach students business skills and how to save and manage their money. I enrolled right away and in just one year I was able to save seventy-seven U.S. dollars in the school bank. At the end of the year, I used some of those funds to set up a small *raspadilla* [snow cone] stand near my school. On my very first day in business, I managed to sell everything! Every day I made and sold a little bit more...and every day, I made a profit!

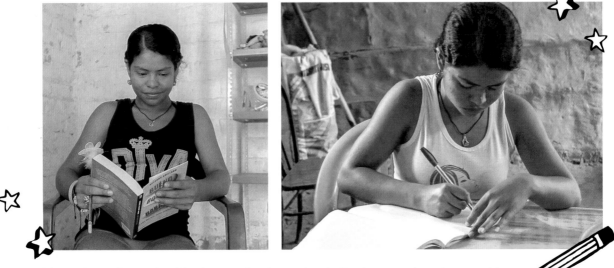

I knew in my heart that I had to get back to school. Getting an education would open new doors — not just for me, but also for my whole family!

It was exciting to see how much money I was able to save, and the snow cone stand is doing very well! Most days I ask my mother to help me set everything up — we have fun working together! I'm proud to be able to earn money for my family when we really need it.

Very soon after I began the raspadilla stand, my father became ill and was no longer able to work. Suddenly I was the person supporting my entire household. This sometimes scares me a little, but I am so proud to be able to do this for my family when they need me. And it is all happening because I was able to go back to school and apply what I learned there to become a businesswoman.

With the earnings I make at the stand, I am able to give my mother money for food, and I can pay for my own school supplies. I am also saving money to pay for further education.

A few short years ago I could not see any way I could get ahead or improve my future. Now I have the skills and knowledge to plan for a bright future for myself and for my family. In the next five years, I want to study and become a great professional. I want to make my parents proud of me!

This is just the beginning...I have big dreams! I'm saving up to go to school for fashion design. I'm going to get ahead and make my parents very proud of me!

Did you know...?

Did you know that countries where girls have less access to education tend to be poorer, while wealthier countries tend to have more gender equality in education?

In such places, young women tend to put 90% of their income into their household! In this way, girls help their families stay healthy and secure and able to educate their children.

Why can educating a *girl* make such a difference?

▶ The more educated a woman is, the healthier her children will be. Girls who receive an education tend to marry later, have fewer children, and are more likely to seek health care for themselves and their children.

▶ An extra year of secondary school increases a girl's potential income by 15–25%

▶ Educating 10% more girls can increase a country's wealth by 3%

**Educate a girl
and she'll benefit
everyone around her**

Sierra Leone

65

Geeta's family in Nepal was so poor that she began working as a house servant when she was just 12. She worked for years, from sunrise until late at night, believing she'd never escape and be free. She earned less than $15 a year!

Now, Geeta is in her 20s and, with support, she has started her own roadside café business where she makes *46 times* more than what she earned as a servant.

Nepal

More than 70 million young people between 15 and 24 years of age are unemployed worldwide. 40 million of those live in Africa.

The Youth in Action project is working to change these statistics! Because unemployment is a worldwide issue, countries must work together to improve their economies.

Young people from half a dozen European and African countries came together in Belgium to discuss Youth Economic Empowerment. They joined important policymakers to talk about the causes and results of youth unemployment, and to look for global solutions.

For Fati, her local Youth Microfinance project is about confidence and independence.

"Before this project, I didn't have a job. I had to ask my husband for money. But now I have my savings and I can contribute to the education of my children."

She joined the project so that she could save a little money to start a small business, but now Fati is the president of the savings group!

Women and girls are also breaking barriers by stepping into careers that have usually been reserved for men in order to make a living. Jeanne is a welder in Benin, and Gloria Joyce works as an auto mechanic in Juba, South Sudan.

Education leads to higher wages, smaller and healthier families, reduced risk of HIV, and more involvement in politics and decision-making.

Jeanne (Benin)

Gloria Joyce (South Sudan)

Educate a girl, and she'll break the endless cycle of poverty!

HAKIMA

Uganda

When we were young, my brothers and sisters and I loved to listen to the stories and fables my mother always told us. Sometimes I remember this one about the tortoise and the birds. One day, a tortoise heard about a party that was happening on the moon, and he convinced the birds to lend him some feathers so that he could go with them. When they arrived on the moon, the tortoise ended up eating everything at the feast, leaving nothing for the birds. The angry birds took back their feathers and left, and the helpless tortoise fell from the sky, cracking his shell. It's supposed to be a story that explains how a tortoise looks, but I think it's a story about power. The tortoise thought it was easy to control the birds, to trick them and take advantage of them. But he had no idea how smart and strong the birds were, and that his journey was impossible without them.

In Uganda, it is easy for those who think they have power to make girls feel helpless. I look around and see girls who are not allowed to go to school and girls who are victims of violence when they do go to class. I hear about girls being forced into marriage. Many of the children here — boys and girls alike — are often caned, burned, or slapped. All of these horrible things are happening because someone decided that girls are not equal — and that they would have more power if they controlled us. This needs to change...and we can be the ones to change it!

Even though I am young, I know I have power. I am very lucky to be able to go to

Did you know...

If all the girls of Uganda completed even just primary school, they would add 13% to their country's total annual income. And if they completed secondary school, that number would jump to a 34% increase in their country's income during their lifetimes!

It was really exciting to travel to New York and to attend the Commission on the Status of Women at the United Nations! I met girls from many different countries, and we had the chance to speak to global leaders about the changes they can make to empower girls around the world.

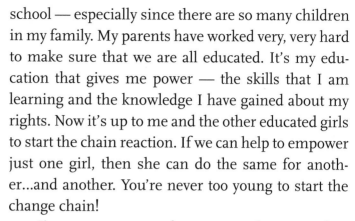

school — especially since there are so many children in my family. My parents have worked very, very hard to make sure that we are all educated. It's my education that gives me power — the skills that I am learning and the knowledge I have gained about my rights. Now it's up to me and the other educated girls to start the chain reaction. If we can help to empower just one girl, then she can do the same for another...and another. You're never too young to start the change chain!

For many years my dream was to become a doctor. I have twelve brothers and sisters, and I think of them coming into this world and how I want my mother to be treated when she gives birth. Many mothers die in childbirth in my village, and even more children die before we can celebrate their first birthday. Some of the babies' illnesses are very easy to treat if you have the knowledge, and I want to be able to help them! But lately I've been realizing that I could make a lot of change — in my country, and maybe even around the world — if I became a lawyer. I've seen and heard about so many cases of violence against girls and women. I want to help them to fight for their rights in court, and to rewrite laws to keep them safe. I've been lucky to have others invest in me, and making sure that girls feel safe and respected is just one way I can pay back what's been given to me!

Education is power! We need to work together to make it possible for every girl to go to school!

Without support from others, I wouldn't have been able to travel to New York to represent children at the fifty-seventh United Nations Commission on the Status of Women. Because someone invested in us, many amazing girls from around the world had the chance to speak with important decision-making members of the United Nations. The clubs and programs I've joined have connected me to others who want to make change and given me information and communication skills that I can use for life. Now it's up to me to use these tools and the power they give me to fight for the rights of girls everywhere!

Here I am doing an interview for United Nations radio! This was a great chance to help people understand the challenges that girls are facing in my country. We all have the power to share our story — where will you share yours?

Did you know...?

For every dollar spent to help people in poor countries, girls receive less than 2 cents.

Worldwide, girls face overwhelming odds from the moment they are born. They can be malnourished, denied an education, and forced into slavery or early marriage.

Helping girls equally is the key to changing lives and transforming

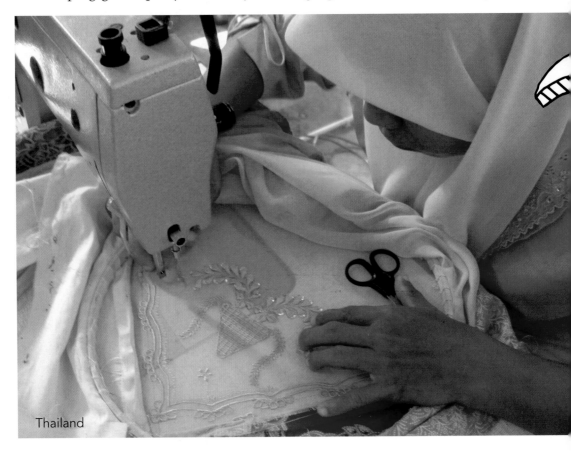

Thailand

communities. Equal access to health care, education, protection, independence, and opportunities to participate in society can break the cycle of poverty.

Spending money on scholarships, safe schools and dormitories, women's health issues, life skills, job training, how to manage income, and small business loans can make huge changes in the life of a girl — and her community. She will return that support many times over.

When the village of Ban Bangyai in Thailand lost all of its fishing boats to the 2004 tsunami, the women and girls came together to form their own business. They wanted to sew head-scarves for the mainly Muslim community.

The Women's Hijab Group was soon created, and with help, they were able to purchase 10 industrial sewing machines and raw materials to start their company.

Simple solutions can help in big ways

Kenya

Giving a girl a food ration when she goes to school keeps her in school and encourages her parents to make her education a priority for the family.

Timor Leste

Giving a mother a small loan to start a business raises her status as an income earner and means she'll reinvest her earnings in her children's education, transforming a cycle of poverty into a cycle of opportunity.

Benin

Giving a girl training in media and a chance to broadcast her views raises her voice within the community and plants the seeds of change.

Because I am a girl...
I will take what you invest in me and uplift everyone around me.

Young people in West Africa are rarely heard from in and by the media. With help, a project called Girls Making Media was created to change this. In the program, children are trained to produce quality information about girls' rights. The program also works with adult journalists to improve their coverage of girls' issues.

The club members receive basic training in media skills — how to gather, write, and report the news. More importantly, they receive training in the areas of child rights, life skills, advocacy (being able to speak about a topic or argue in favor of something), sexual and reproductive health, and group organization. Then, by sharing what they know, they are able to empower others in their communities.

79

Bangladesh

Beauty Roy (right) was taken out of school several times over the course of her education. Each time she had to overcome financial obstacles and family pressure in order to get back into the classroom. When she was finally able to return, she rose to the top of her class!

Now Beauty is a community healthcare worker. Not only does she help to care for many people in her village, she is now able to support herself and her family. She also encourages the parents in her community to keep their children in school!

Burkina Faso

Malika (right) was born in the U.S. and lived there until she was 4 years old. Her mother's job took them to Tunisia, and now they live in Burkina Faso, where she is in the 8th grade.

When Malika learned that there were girls in the rural areas who had to walk more than 9 miles (14 km) each way to school every day, she and a few friends decided that they wanted to do something. They decided to raise money so that they could provide bicycles for some of the girls.

After three months of hard work, they had raised enough to donate 60 bicycles!

When we protect the rights of girls, we can make sure that they have everything from education to health care. When access to every opportunity is equal for girls, we can all work together to create a better world!

FAHMEEDA

Canada

Fahmeeda is a Youth Ambassador *for*

Plan Canada and a member of the Because I am a Girl Speaker's Bureau. She speaks several times a month at schools and community events, both in her city and across Canada. She has also started her own organization called Youth for Humanity. One of her new goals is to continue her current research on human trafficking and to protect the rights of women and youth around the world.

I was born in Islamabad, the capital of Pakistan, but my family moved to Canada when I was nine. I have spent half my life in each country. When I was thirteen I traveled back to Pakistan for a visit that changed me forever. Even though I'd experienced daily life in two very different countries, I can honestly say that I didn't know a lot about the barriers girls face around the world.

In Pakistan, a huge flood had pushed people out of their homes and separated many families. I volunteered at a shelter that had been set up to help women and children. Everyone who lived there — including the kids — had to work to pay for their stay in the shelter. Every morning I felt sick to my stomach as I watched groups of children heading into a factory, where they would spend all day working. They should have been on their way to school!

I made friends with a girl at the shelter who was about eight months pregnant. She'd never been to a doctor. When it came time to have the baby, there were problems during the delivery, and she didn't survive the birth. I was heartbroken, but I was also really angry. She died because she had no medical care, and her baby was now an orphan.

I returned to Canada with a fire inside me. I had to do something!

We stayed in a hotel that was also a vocational training school — all of the workers there were students learning valuable management and tourism skills!

One of my favorite moments from my trip to Tanzania was meeting the women's microfinance group. Whenever one of the women bought a share, it was written down on the chart, and the other women would chant and clap with joy.

I began searching online to learn more about human rights and social justice, especially issues affecting women and children. And that's when I found Because I am a Girl! I started a Because I am a Girl club at my school, and joined the organization's Speaker's Bureau, which helped me a lot with my communication and speaking skills. I was really very shy when I was younger. Now I feel much more confident! It also connected me with many new people, people who became friends and who want to make change, just like me.

Hearing the stories of other girls from other countries helps us all to understand that we have a lot in common. We may face different challenges, but we all have hopes and dreams.

Fahmeeda in Tanzania

When I was invited on a trip to Tanzania as a youth delegate to learn about youth entrepreneurship and microfinance projects there, I was so proud! Traveling to Africa was another life-changing experience. When we sat down with a women's savings and loan group in a local village, I met a young woman who had started out by taking a loan to create a soap-making business. Now she has her own factory and imports and exports soap all over the place! It was wonderful to see the women overcoming many barriers, and then frustrating to see them blocked by others. When we asked them, "What is the hardest thing about being a woman in your village?" we were a little surprised by the answer: finding firewood — a role that is still almost exclusively a female one. Without firewood, water can't be boiled and food can't be cooked. If the nearby forests are private, there is nowhere to collect wood. And there is no one to fight the unjust laws that have allowed public forests to become private property.

I was one of more than six hundred youth delegates from across the world to attend the United Nations Youth Takeover Conference in New York in July of 2013. We created a youth-led resolution on education that would be presented to the UN General Assembly. As part of the youth takeover, the United Nations had declared Malala Yousafzai's birthday

Meeting with Ahmad Alhendawi (the UN Envoy for Youth) was such an amazing experience. It was so empowering to know our voices were being heard!

(July 12th) to be Malala Day, and she was coming to the UN to speak publicly for the first time since she had been shot by the Taliban.

When I first heard Malala speak, I had goosebumps. I was in awe when she started, and in awe when she finished! I felt a very special connection because we were born in the same country, but you could feel something happening in that room — everyone was linked and standing proud with her! When Malala said she was "just one among the many girls that fight and advocate for girls' rights," it really stuck with me. There are millions of "Malalas" — girls who face all sorts of different barriers that prevent them from going to school. But that can change too. Like Malala says, it all starts with "...one child, one teacher, one pen, and one book."

If I had any advice for girls around the world, it would be to believe that you have the power to make change, and that power starts with your voice. It's okay to be angry about injustices. Find your own passion — and talk about it with everyone who will listen. For me, it's that no more girls should die in childbirth because of a lack of simple medical care. For me, it's that children who must work should have decent work that also allows them to go to school. For me, it's that not one more girl is harmed simply because she wants to go to school. For me, it's that poor people should have lawyers who can advocate for their rights. I want to go to university so that I am equipped to deal with some of these problems. I am lucky because I have many people supporting me. Everything good that happens in this world starts with one person wanting things to change, wanting things to be better and sticking with it until the job is done. I know I can change the world and so can you.

Did you know...?

Every day, girls prove that they can make a difference, even when problems seem too big to solve. Here are just a few examples of how girls are raising their voices to change the world. They are the leaders who inspire others to take action and bring equality to girls everywhere. The more people who join in, the smaller the problems become.

Vietnam

These girls in Vietnam come together to discuss gender issues and what they can do together at their life skills club.

Egypt

These girls in Cairo, Egypt are mapping the riskiest and safest routes for girls to take when traveling in their community.

Denmark

Youth journalists Reina (Indonesia) and Beatrice (Kenya) attended the United Nations Climate Change Conference in Copenhagen — where they challenged world leaders to describe their plans to tackle climate change.

Reina, Indonesia

Beatrice, Kenya

These girls are members of a children's club in their village in India, and have been trained in "child media" to write reports, take photos, produce radio shows, and create cartoons to explain and teach about issues in their community.

India

These girls have traveled to the United States from countries around the world, to participate in and learn how to stand up for what they believe in at the Youth United for Global Action and Awareness (YUGA) Conference.

United States

Philippines

In some areas of the Philippines that were the hardest hit by Typhoon Haiyan, "junior news crews" were given flip cameras. This helped them to express their needs and opinions to the rest of the world in a creative and powerful way.

Rwanda

Petitions and letters to government officials were a huge part of informing the United Nations about the need for a Day of the Girl!

Zimbabwe

Liberia

I Am A Girl
e THERE, include

Kenneth is the Vice President of the Girls Making Media project in his village in Liberia. He knows that boys and girls are equal and should be treated fairly, and he talks about that in his radio broadcasts. Boys and men are important messengers when they speak up for gender equality.

Girls in Chipinge, Zimbabwe gave powerful speeches about the importance of stopping child marriages in their community.

Students at Secord Elementary
School in Toronto, Canada, are
sharing their letters to Malala
Yousafzai with her father, Ziauuddin.
Their message? You inspire us, and
together we are stronger.

Canada

You Can Change the World!

Now that you've met some girls who are changing the world they live in, you can see why taking action, speaking out, and standing up for what's right is just what we should all do when things are unfair.

Sometimes it is hard to see how you fit in when it comes to making change. When the numbers and problems are so large, it is easy to be discouraged. As just one person in a world of more than seven billion, how do *you* begin?

The girls in this book show you the way. Often, others are just waiting for someone like you to take the first step. Getting them to join you can make things both easier and more powerful. Your tools are your mind, your hands, and your voice. Do what is safe, what makes sense, and what feels right.

The next time you hear yourself thinking or saying, "This is wrong, someone should do something," look in the mirror. That "someone" could be you!

Photo Credits

ROSEMARY MCCARNEY leads the Plan International Canada team where she helped create the Because I am a Girl initiative and worked to have October 11th declared the International Day of the Girl by the United Nations.

JEN ALBAUGH is a former elementary school teacher and librarian currently working as a freelance writer and editor in Toronto who is greatly inspired by the work of Plan and the Because I am a Girl initiative.

PLAN INTERNATIONAL is one of the world's oldest and largest international charities, working in partnership with millions of people around the world to end global poverty. Not for profit, independent, and inclusive of all faiths and cultures, Plan has only one agenda: to improve the lives of children.